PAWS OF WISDOM

Valuable Lessons We Can Learn from Our Pets

Sofia Steryo-Bartmus

Let this book touch your heart and inspire you to make your own changes from the inside out.

Best Wishes

Soifer

PAWS OF WISDOM

Paws of Wisdom
Valuable Lessons We Can Learn from Our Pets

Publisher: Harmony Book Publishing
21900 Londelius Street
West Hills, CA 91304
Phone: (818) 456-5193
Toll-Free: (877) 585-9553
Fax: (818) 888-8594
Email: harmonybookpub@quixnet.net

ISBN: 0-9770955-0-9
Library of Congress Control Number: 2005932258

First Edition
Printed in he United States of America
10 9 8 7 6 5 4 3 2 1

This book is dedicated to Bunny ,
The best little puppy
in the whole wide world...
Her life has been an inspiration.

February 1985 - November 1999

Acknowledgments

I want to thank my husband, Galen, for encouraging me to write. He believed in me more than I believed in myself. He never gave up on me. He helped me throughout the entire process with his invaluable input and constant support.

Table of Contents

Foreword

I thank God for the beloved animals that share our homes and our lives. They demand so little—a word, a pat, a walk in the park, a bowl of food. Yet, they give us so much. They give us soothing warmth, loyal company and unconditional affection. Our responsibility is to return their love and devotion with faithful care and gentle kindness.

I am thankful for having had the privilege to have loved and shared my life with a couple of special pets, especially our little "dog daughter" or "paws," as we affectionately called Bunny. She brought our family a lot of laughter and happiness along with sadness and grief.

While, observing our little "puppy" (we called her that a lot, even when she was up in years) she taught us many lessons which can be applied to our every day lives. I never really thought about it much when she was alive, but after she was gone, I started remembering things she did. Not a day goes by without realizing the lessons that she taught me. Although we cannot communicate with our pets verbally, I do believe that we form bonds that sometimes go beyond verbal communications. These bonds touch our senses in a much deeper level.

This is her story… I hope you will find it entertaining, touching and sometimes thought provoking. It will make you smile, laugh and sometimes even cry. My wish is that it will touch the hearts of many, even those of you who have never owned a pet.

"…and God created…
every living creature…
and God saw that it was good…"
<u>Genesis 1:21</u>

BUNNY'S STORY

One early Saturday morning in February, 1985, my mother, my then "future" mother-in-law and I met for breakfast and then went shopping. While shopping we saw a litter of puppies that the cashier had brought in to give away. We were told they were six weeks old. There were six black puppies, and one whose color was tan. All the puppies were sleeping except the tan one. This one was pretty active. I could not resist picking her up.

Since my parents had lost their dog, Lucky, two years prior, we tried to convince my mother that she and dad needed a new puppy. At first she resisted, but finally she gave in and we took the puppy home and named her Bunny.

Bunny lived with my parents for about a year until my parents moved in with me. So that's when I started to know Bunny better and get closer to her. I started doing more and more things with her and for her. (Later, when I got married, Bunny found a "special" bond with my husband.)

Bunny's Wisdom:

Listen to your parents and don't ever run out into the street, you can get hurt

Bunny's first experience with the vet came on a day we had a house warming party at my house. As the last guests were leaving, Bunny ran into the street, and the next thing we knew she was hit by a car. She was not hurt, but pretty shook up. Nevertheless, we took her to the emergency room to make sure.

**Here we go again! What am I doing here?
Didn't I see Mr. Doctor last week already?**

The next big episode came in November 1986. One day I noticed she was shaking while sleeping. The next day she started vomiting. She was diagnosed by the doctor as going through an "adrenal crisis." Adrenal crisis requires prompt IV administration of hydrocortisone and saline solution. With proper treatment the crisis subsides quickly. The doctor took a lot of blood and urine tests and determined that Bunny was suffering from Addison's disease. After a week in the hospital, Bunny returned home and was put on cortisosteriod replacement, with cortisone and hydrocortisone medications to be taken for life. After this incident, Bunny always became prone to infections and stayed in the hospital on several occasions.

It's no fun being sick…………..

Addison's disease occurs when 90 percent of the adrenal gland is destroyed. This is caused by an imbalance of the electrolytes; decreased sodium and increased potassium. It normally occurs in people, very seldom in animals. The patient experiences weakness, fatigue, nausea, vomiting and often dehydration. There is a decreased tolerance of even minor stress. That's why 4th of July became a dreaded holiday for all of us, because Bunny would stress out with the loud noises. She would bark non-stop and run around as soon as the fireworks began. Then she would start vomiting. We always ended up taking her to the doctor the following day. We had tried tranquilizers, but they did not work.

On July 6th 1989 she became very ill again, and the doctor said that the pills alone would no longer work for her. In addition to the pills, which she was taking every other day, we also started her on experimental injections. At the time, since this was not routine treatment for animals,

I don't feel so good...

we signed release forms authorizing the doctor to administer this treatment. We were told that this procedure may or may not benefit Bunny, and could even result in death. However, if we didn't try it, she would die that week in the hospital. So, we chose to put her on these injections, which she had to get every 28 days without fail, for the rest of her life.

Bunny was almost 15 years old when she died on November 6, 1999.

FOLLOW YOUR HUNCHES

Most Often They Will Lead You To The Right Decisions

"People cannot see the whole scope of God's work from beginning to end"
Ecclesiastics 3:11

Attempt to make wise decisions. Sometimes we cannot see the big picture, but I believe that God can, and he is working everything out for our ultimate good. When you have a "hunch" or a "feeling" about something, go ahead and follow through with it. It is your intuition and God's way of telling you. Unfortunately, what most people do instead is ignore their inner voice and their hunches.

If you insist in seeing everything perfectly clear before you decide, you will never decide. Sometimes you need to go with your "hunch."

The decision to take Bunny home probably meant life or death for her. Most other people might have chosen to put her to sleep after finding out her medical condition. Although my mother was totally against getting a new dog, there was something in me that said I had to convince her to take the puppy.

She had a lot of energy and a personality. She was different. Little did I know at the time what the future would hold.

The other decision we had to make was when she was about five years old. As I mentioned earlier, the medication she had been on was no longer effective. We had to start giving her monthly injections in addition to her pills. At the time the drug was used only on humans and we had to sign an agreement to try it on Bunny. I did not feel we had a choice. We either tried it or she died. Period. She was able to live another 10 years. Although she was fragile and always needed special care, we enjoyed having her.

The decision we made to keep her alive gave us years of companionship, love, fun times, laughter and a lot of compassion. She probably did more for us than we did for her. When my dad was ill, she would sit next to him and keep him company for hours. I also feel that God sent her to me to ease the loss of several babies that I was not able to carry to term. With Bunny, I went through all the different emotions of disappointment, love, anger and worry that a mother has for a child. I felt a special bond with her that I had never experienced with anyone else before. When my husband and I got married, he became Bunny's "favorite." He took her for walks and he played with her gently, just perfect for her pace. He later told me that Bunny had prepared him for the long suffering and death of his father.

"A wise man makes his own decisions, an ignorant man follows the public opinion"

Chinese proverb

Bunny had touched us all in a special way, family and friends alike. She loved seeing and being with our friends, and they would treat her and talk to her as if she were human. Many of our friends enjoyed staying with Bunny, when we would be out of town. If we had decided not to keep her, we would have missed out on all of that, and all that she taught us. What a loss that would have been for all whose lives she touched.

"We make our decisions, and then our decisions turn around and make us"

F. W. Foremen

Bunny's most important contribution was to the medical field, since she took part in an experiment, which would help other animals with Addison's disease in the future. Her doctor kept monthly records, which were being reported to the pharmaceutical company. So, I feel that her life not only touched humans but also attributed to the future well being of other pets.

ACCEPT PEOPLE AND THINGS AS THEY ARE

*"Preference becomes prejudice
when we refuse to see the good
in anything we happen to dislike"*
C. E. Katerndahl

Bunny did not prejudge anybody. If she met them for the first time, she would sniff and make sure they were OK to be in the house. Once they passed the test, she would treat them as one of the family. She may have had a few "favorite" friends, but as long as people played with her, gave her treats and were kind to her, she liked them. It did not matter if they had a disability or if they spoke a different language (actually, since my parents spoke Greek to Bunny, she would respond to both Greek and English). She didn't care about their race, color or age.

I also learned to accept her with all of her problems and her somewhat neurotic personality. We treated her as a "normal," healthy dog.

I realized that as we go through life, we meet people with different personalities, disabilities,

> *"Distinguished men are hard to find in a crowd, because they usually look so undistinguished"*
> **William Feather**

cultures, ethnic and socio-economic backgrounds, sexual orientation or religious beliefs. I asked myself: Am I tolerant and accepting of people who are "different"? or am I only associating with people who are like me? Do I pre-judge people based on their appearance or a certain behavior? What if I caught them on an "off" day. Maybe they are going through a life crisis or a tragedy. In the process I learned to get to know people better before dismissing them from my life. I learned to work with each one and allow them the same opportunity to express their individuality that I desire for myself. I now enjoy the beauty and benefit in diversity.

> *"Man looks on the outward appearance, but God looks on the heart."*
> **The Bible**

- Be reminded that the fat, squirmy caterpillar becomes a beautiful butterfly

- Work on being more open and accepting; you may be pleasantly surprised at what wonderful experiences you may encounter

- Seek the good in others and refrain from criticism, offering praise and gratitude

🐕 Learn to appreciate the differences in people and learn from them

---

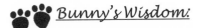 *Bunny's Wisdom:*

Work on getting along with all kinds of people

APPRECIATE WHAT YOU HAVE

Learn To Enjoy The Simple Things In Life

*B*unny was always happy with simple things such as a hug, a kiss, a pat on the head, a warm bed, and of course, a snack. Although there were days when she felt lousy, she made the best out of the good days. She seemed to cope well with her condition.

 Bunny's Wisdom:

- *Delight in the simple joy of a long walk*

- *Allow the experience of fresh air and the wind in your face to be pure ecstasy*

- *Wag your tail and say "thank you" for all the "doggie" treats*

- *Who needs a big home entertainment system? A bone or an old shoe can entertain me for hours*

- *Every garbage can looks like a cold buffet to me*

THANK YOU!!!

How many of us take things for granted? We sometimes want what we don't have, instead of being thankful and appreciating what we do have. Jay Winner, M.D. author of *Stress Management Made Simple*, explains that reflecting on all that you have, instead of on what you don't have will decrease stress. Many times we hear people talking about "the Good Ol' Days." Thirty years from now, we will be talking about the "Good Ol' Days." So guess what! Today is the "good old days."

Many people's lives are shattered by pain and illness, and yet often times those who suffer have re-evaluated their lives by reaching into their depths to discover what is most valuable in life and are content and at peace. Let's learn from them and not take for granted the miracle of our intricately functioning bodies. Let us learn to enjoy every single day that we are alive and well.

Make it a point to appreciate and enjoy the little things. If you are thankful for the little things, just imagine how great you will feel for the bigger things. Things don't always have to be expensive or elaborate to be worthwhile. How about:

- A moment in the sun
- Having lunch or a phone conversation with a friend
- A walk on the beach
- A kiss from a loved one
- A sermon
- Your favorite song
- A manicure, a pedicure or a massage
- Reading a good book

There are countless wonders and simple miracles that await us. The reason we do not notice them is because we are too preoccupied with other things. All we need to do is start each day with a commitment to be aware of the wonderful things and people around us.

Work on cultivating your ability to see the extraordinary in everyday living.

Don't know where to start? How about doing some simple things, such as:

🐾 Setting aside a few minutes each day to contemplate just one wonderful thing in your life

🐾 Turning off the noise and distractions around you. Silence will stimulate your thoughts and imagination.

🐾 Taking a walk in a peaceful park

🐾 Spending quiet time with someone you love

🐾 Listening to soothing music

🐾 Spending time in prayer and meditation.

🐾 Develop an "attitude of gratitude"

"The deepest principles in human nature is the craving to be appreciated"
William James

🐾 Say "thank you" to everyone for everything they do for you

🐾 Appreciate your parents, your children, your spouse and your friends

"He who can no longer pause to wonder and stand rapt in awe, is as good as dead: his eyes are closed."
Albert Einstein

🐾 Appreciate each day that you are alive and well

🐾 Learn to be joyful with what God has given you, instead of being bitter about what you don't have

**Thank GOD I get to sleep in the bedroom
instead of outside in the cold "Doggie House"...**

*"Gratitude is not only the greatest of virtues
but the parent of all the others."*

Marcus T. Cicero

BE KIND AND GENTLE TO ALL LIVING THINGS

"Make yourself a blessing to someone. Your kind smile or pat on the back just might pull someone back from the edge"
Carmelia Elliott

once read a quote from Andy Rooney. He wrote:"The average dog is a nicer person than the average person." Well, maybe there is some truth to it. Maybe our goal in life is to try to be as good a person as our dogs already think we are. They always think we are the best, no matter how we treat them.

Bunny instinctively knew when someone in the family was not feeling well. When my father was sick, she would sit by his feet for hours, to keep him company. She was repaying him for all the long, long walks he would take her on every day. The ones where he would let her sniff for hours. I don't know how he found the patience. Just before he passed away, he would stay in bed for long periods of time.

Bunny would jump up on the bed and stay with him until it was time for her dinner.

I know how you feel...............

Occasionally when she would see a tear in my eye, she would come and try to lick my face. She wanted to comfort me, in the only way she knew how.

> *"There is no psychiatrist in the world*
> *like a puppy licking your face"*
> **Ben Williams**

When she sensed that something was wrong, she would leave us alone and not ask for a walk or pester us to play with her.

Like our pets we should also be sensitive to others and be as kind as possible.

🐾 Show kindness to people you meet. You don't know what their day has been like. You may be the only person who is kind to them

🐾 Ask yourself how you would want others to treat you and then act accordingly

🐾 Encourage people and be a blessing to others

🐾 Give someone a compliment

> *A kind word is never lost...*
> **Proverbs**

> *"Kindness is a language which the deaf can hear and the blind can read"*
> **Mark Twain**

🐾 Smile. Make it a point to start your day with a smile. I am sure you can find something in your life to smile about. Your smile can make a difference in someone's life, and it's free to give away

🐾 Begin each day by reading a book of daily devotions or inspirational quotes to get you in a positive frame of mind

🐕 Do whatever works for you to get you into a good mood (exercise, play your favorite music, listen to your favorite radio program)

"Treat people as if they were what they ought to be and you help them to become what they are capable of being"
Johann W. von Goethe

"Be kind. Remember, everyone you meet is fighting a hard battle"
T. H. Thompson

 Bunny's Wisdom:

- *When someone is having a bad day sit close and be silent*
- *If someone looks sad, kiss him in the face*

BE CONSISTENT

*B*unny was consistent with things that she did. We always knew what to expect. For example: Every morning around 3 or 4 a.m., she would scratch the door to go out. Upon her return she would jump on our bed, as my husband was closing the door, and lay on his spot. When asked to move, she would reluctantly move slightly over to the middle of the bed where she would sleep the rest of the night.

Bunny was also "consistently" disobedient, due to, I might add, my being "inconsistent" with her discipline. I had developed the bad habit of not disciplining Bunny the correct way. When she would do something bad, sometimes I would scold her and sometimes I would not. I would give her mixed signals. Or, I would scold her briefly, and then, I would hug and kiss her. This resulted in reinforcing the wrong behavior.

I learned that when we discipline a pet, just as with a child, we must be consistent. We must follow through with what we promised to do, otherwise it does not mean anything. When we say one thing and do something else, after a while they don't take us seriously.

🐕 When you discipline, be firm and
consistent. They must know that you
mean what you say

We must also be consistent with things we do in
our daily life. We are consistent in going to work
everyday, then why not be consistent with everything
else we do on a daily basis? When I am inconsistent I
am unpredictable. People around me are uneasy.
They don't know how to "read" me or what to expect.

🐕 Don't be hot one moment and cold the
next. Don't go up and down. The ups
and downs zap your energy and your
joy

🐾🐾 *Bunny's Wisdom:*

- *When I know that you will follow
-through with your threats, I
obey*

- *If my behavior is predictable,
people don't need to guess what I
will do next or how I will react to
a situation*

BE HUMBLE

"Apart from Me, you can do nothing"
John 15:4

Bunny depended on us for everything. She happily received what we lovingly provided for her. I remember one time I had changed (with the doctor's permission) the frequency of her medication. I thought she was doing pretty well, so I gave her the pills every three days instead of every day. On the third day I took her for a walk, only to discover that after walking five minutes her legs gave out and she could no longer walk. Her back legs were paralyzed. I'll never forget the look on her face. (Not to mention the panic I felt!). She did not know what had happened to her, but she knew she was helpless. I carried her home and never tried to play doctor again. As she got older she also became even more dependent on us. We had to help her get up on the couch, the bed and even the stairs. She had to humble herself, and let us help her do things.

I learned that as we get older we get humbled. We are not able to do all the things we used to do. I experienced it with my parents as well as Bunny. It made me realize that I had no control over certain situations. Our lives can change in a split second. One day you are well and the next you have an accident or an incurable medical condition. We just need to deal with it the best we can and live with it.

- 🐕 Don't take things for granted
- 🐕 Don't be arrogant about what you have…it can be taken away from you in a moment's notice
- 🐕 Don't let your pride and prosperity get in the way of being humble

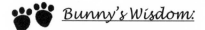 *Bunny's Wisdom:*

I let my family help me with the things I can no longer do myself

BE PATIENT

"Patience is the companion of wisdom"
St. Augustine

unny demonstrated a lot of patience. When she smelled a gopher, she would sit and wait by the hole for hours for the gopher to appear. Sometimes we had to pry her away since there was no gopher coming out. Other times she would nudge her leash with her nose, which hung on the doorknob. This was her signal to us that she wanted to go out. Then she would sit by the door and wait, and wait and wait. She did many other things that showed her patience. In the end, if she waited long enough, Bunny would get what she wanted.

"Patience is a tree whose roots is bitter, but its fruit is very sweet"
Chinese Proverb

Impatience has always been something I have struggled with. I always want things to happen RIGHT NOW. It is something I have had to work on. I could never understand how people can be so slow, and not understand something right away or get things done on time. With time I have learned that I cannot always have what I want when I want it.

When someone you love is ill, or has a disability, you have to be on their timetable, and you can't be impatient. They usually move slower, they eat slower, they bathe slower, they don't want to play, they don't want to eat, they don't want to do the things you want to do with them. They want to rest. But why are we so impatient anyway? Why do we want things to happen RIGHT NOW?

"We can rejoice, when we run into problems, for we know that they are good for us—they help us learn to be patient"
Romans 5:3

"With time and patience the mulberry leaf becomes a silk gown"
Chinese Proverb

There are other things that make us impatient: the weight we put on may not come off as fast as we want it to. The promotion we want may not come our way fast enough. We may not find the mate or have children when we think we should. We may not afford to buy all the luxuries we want when we want them. We must have patience. We may not understand why we don't get things when we want them but there is always a reason. Whether we realize it or not things happen at the right time.

I learned that it is more important to stay close to the ones you love and give them comfort when they need it…other things can wait. Things don't matter as much as we think they do…people matter.

I learned that if you keep going in the right direction, in due time you will get what you want.

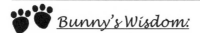 *Bunny's Wisdom:*

> *If you are patient, you can get what you want*

BE YOURSELF

*"Until you make peace with who you are,
you will never be content with what you have"*
<u>Doris Mortman</u>

Bunny taught me how to really be myself and let go. I was not threatened in any way, and I was not afraid of being rejected. Therefore, I could laugh, play, cry and feel free. She brought out different emotions in me that I always kept back when around people. I did not have to pretend and put up a front. She brought out the child in me. I felt she loved me just for being with her, just for being me, as I did with her. We had total trust with each other. Bunny trusted me because she knew I would never do anything that would harm her and that I would protect her from harm. My love for her was unconditional and so was hers for me. I accepted her with all her imperfections. She did not need to pretend to be something she was not.

She was unique. We are unique too with many flaws and yet God loves us anyway.

🐾 Don't pretend to be different from what you really are

🐾 Don't be concerned only with what other people see on the outside

As we grow older we tend to leave behind our spontaneity or innocence and start presenting a person other than our true self. We do not want to get "hurt." Well, I think when we do that, we miss out on love, friendships and closeness with other people. Remember, everyone has similar hurts, "bad childhood experiences," or other unpleasant circumstances. If you don't open up to share yours, they will not open up either and you will end up with a superficial relationship.

Start enjoying true and close relationships with your family and friends—it will make all the difference in the world. Do you want to go through life pretending you are somebody that you are not? If you do that, how can you trust others?

> *"You may be deceived if you trust too much,*
> *but you will live in torment*
> *if you do not trust enough"*
> **Dr. Frank Crane**

🐾 If you are honest with people they will be honest with you

🐕 Share yourself with others and they will share with you

🐕 Learn to love the child inside you. It will not be easy at first. However, when you are yourself, you will attract real friends and they will love you for who you are

> *"The great pleasure of a dog is that you make a fool of yourself with him and not only he will not scold you, but he will make a fool of himself, too"*
> **Samuel Butler, Notebooks, 1912**

 Bunny's Wisdom:

- *Share yourself with others*
- *Don't pretend to be something you're not, just be you*

**I can sleep on my back, with my belly exposed
because I feel totally secure with my family**

*"Always to distrust is an error,
as well as always to trust..."*

<u>Goethe</u>

CLEANLINESS IS ESSENTIAL

Bunny would sit and lick herself clean constantly. Although she hated taking a bath, she always felt better afterwards. She would shake off the water and run around, jumping for joy. We'd all take turns giving her a bath, however, my mother was the one who did it the most. As soon as Bunny would see my mother bring out the bucket of water, shampoo, brush and towel, she would run away and hide. We would call her and call her and it would take a while before she would reluctantly reappear from her hiding place. She knew it was only a matter of time before we would find her and drag her outside.

Once she was clean and dry she looked beautiful. Once a month she would also get what we called a "pedicure." The vet would cut her toenails. She never allowed us to do it after I accidentally cut a little of her quick, but she sat patiently with the vet when he did it. Anyway, she felt better when she was groomed and clean.

We as humans also feel better on the inside when we know we look good and smell good on the outside. And when we feel good on the inside it makes us more radiant and more pleasant for others to be around us. So, I think it is important that we take care of our hygiene and personal grooming.

Bunny's Wisdom:

- *Make sure you don't have "doggie" breath*

- *Taking a bath was never my favorite thing to do, but I loved the results*

- *Stay well groomed so that people will enjoy petting you and want to be around you*

- *Cleanliness is critical. Always lick yourself clean*

Why ME?

After my bath I look and feel soooo pretty ....

COMMUNICATE

"If you want a response,
you have to ask for it"
John Huenefeld

Although dogs cannot talk, they can let you know what they want or how they feel by the way they behave. If Bunny didn't feel good or didn't want to cuddle or play, she would growl a little or show her teeth in an aggressive way. She didn't need to speak. I could read the "cues." I had to pay attention and listen to her. Listening is part of communicating. If we listened more and talked less we would probably clear up a lot of misunderstandings. The better listeners we become the better our relationships will be with our family, friends, employees, business partners or bosses.

🐕 Learn to understand the "cues" and act accordingly

🐕 Learn to listen to what people are saying to you

There is a big difference between hearing and listening. I believe we all need to master the following listening skills:

🐕 Let the speaker finish. Interrupting is the most common listening offense. Finishing someone's thought or asking too many questions bugs the speaker, and can make them clam up

"We have two ears and one tongue in order that we may hear more and speak less"
Diogenes

🐕 Don't multitask. You miss information if you read or type during a chat, and you may offend the speaker. If you're busy, ask if you can talk later and set a time to do so

"I like to listen. I have learned a great deal from listening carefully. Most people never listen..."
Ernest Hemingway

Communication is a two-way street. I also had to communicate to her what I wanted from her, or that I was too busy to play. We need to let others know how we feel and what we want. People cannot read our mind.

"Speak little, do much...."
Benjamin Franklin

🐕 Communicate your needs and ask for
what you want

The fact that Bunny did not always get what she
wanted, did not stop her from trying. She never
assumed anything. If she wanted a snack or her
dinner, she would lie down in from of my mother and
make little sounds, which if ignored, would escalate
in volume, followed by barking.

**Helloooooo, This is empty!
When do you plan to fill it UP?**

When Bunny wanted to go for a walk, she would
nudge her leash and then jump on my husband's lap.
She would also assert herself when she wanted us to
play with her "favorite" toys.

Here is my leash....
are you ready to take me out for a walk?

Bunny's behavior made me realize that I too must ask for what I want. It made me stop and think. Do I know what I want? and if so, what am I doing about it? How am I fulfilling my dreams and aspirations? Am I taking the necessary steps to reach my goals?

"Ask, and you will be given what you ask for; Seek, and you will find; Knock, and the door will be opened to you"
Matthew 7:7

Do you know what you want? Have you ever thought about it?

🐕 Write down all the things you dream of having, doing, being and then work on a plan to fulfill those dreams

🐾 Write down your dreams even if they seem to be unattainable and don't put limitations on yourself

🐾 Don't sabotage yourself by saying 'why bother"? I can't have it anyway. Who says you can't? Instead ask yourself: Why Not? and What If?

> *"You can get anything—anything you ask for in prayer—if you believe"*
> **Matthew 21:22**

 Bunny's Wisdom:

- *Unless you ask, you don't get*

- *You only get what you expect*

- *Always ask for what you want in a nice way first, if that fails, become more assertive*

Once in a while out of no reason at all, we would ask Bunny to "sit" or do a trick for us. She would give us this look as if to ask: "why?" or she would simply walk away with a look that said: "this doesn't make any sense to me, and I am not going to do it!" She would also get pretty defensive and give a little growl if we dared to come too close to her bowl while she was eating. Do we speak up for what we believe in? When something is a life or death situation we have no problem speaking up, do we? Then what holds us back other times?

- 🐕 Speak out for what you believe in and stop doing things to please others

- 🐕 Do you tell people what they want to hear or how you really feel?

- 🐕 Do you do things even when you don't believe in them?

- 🐕 Express your beliefs. Don't hold back. You may help someone else by doing that. It only takes one person to make a difference

Recipe for Failure: Try to please everyone

Don't you dare come any closer....................

Bunny's Wisdom:

- *Growl to let others know when they have invaded your territory*

- *Let people know when what they are asking you to do, is not making any sense*

Last but not least, let's not forget that we constantly interact with people who come from different cultures and backgrounds. They may speak a different language. What we think they mean and what they actually mean could be a different story.

- Make sure you let others know where you stand, what you want, how you want it. If there is a misunderstanding, explain what you mean

- If you are not sure what the other person wants or means, ask questions to clarify their position

- Find out where they are coming from and the reason for their behavior before you jump to a conclusion

- Don't make up your mind without all the facts

- Communication is the key to any encounter. Many relationships fail because of lack of communication

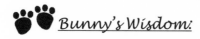 _Bunny's Wisdom:_

Don't bark at the wrong moment,
size up the situation first

CONTROL YOUR ANGER

"Anger is a stone thrown at a wasp's nest"
American Proverb

I still remember the day when I came home from a very stressful day at the office, and found my brand new, favorite shoes chewed up by Bunny. I had spent a lot of time to find that "perfect" pair. I totally lost it. I had never done that before, but I got so mad at her for doing what she did that I spanked her and screamed at her for quite a long time. She really got scared and went hiding and didn't come out for hours. She had never seen me so upset. I

> *"Don't be quick-tempered, for anger is the friend of fools"*
> **Ecclesiastes 7:9**

was so ashamed of myself afterwards. How could I have been so cruel and nasty? I scared myself. I vowed that I would never do that again. How silly it was to loose control over a pair of stupid shoes. I really felt terrible. After all, some of the blame was mine for leaving the shoes close to her reach. I should have known better. After all, puppies will chew anything.

We often lose our temper without evaluating the situation calmly. We end up doing or saying the wrong thing. We react. Afterwards we feel guilty and bad about our behavior, but it is too late. Studies have shown that when we get mad and lose our temper, we actually cause real damage to ourselves.

"When anger rises, think of the consequences"
Confucius

Our mental state produces our physical problems. Our body chemistry changes. If we could always keep our minds in harmony, our bodies would not be sick. Therefore, when we allow our emotions to get out of hand, we actually poison our bodies.

Other times we may show anger in the little things we do and say that are hurtful to others. We say little cutting remarks; we are sarcastic; we belittle others; we say nasty things behind people's backs. These things can ultimately be very destructive to our relationships with people.

"If you are patient in one moment of anger, you will escape a hundred days of sorrow"...
Chinese Proverb

🐕 Don't let anger take control of your life. If you don't control your anger, it will control you

🐕 Don't lose your temper. You may say or do something you will later regret

---

🐾 *Bunny's Wisdom:*

- *Avoid biting when a simple growl will do*

- *Do not go to bed while you are still angry, always make up first*

TAKE FEAR OUT OF YOUR LIFE

*"Nothing in life is to be feared.
It is only to be understood"*

Marie Curie

Bunny was fearful of a lot of things that were not harmful to her. She was afraid of loud noises. Whenever she would hear a loud noise, she would jump on my lap (all 50+ lbs of her) and stay there until the noise would go away. She was afraid of other dogs. She hated going to the doctor's office. She would start shaking uncontrollably once she realized where we were going. A lot of her fears were imagined.

What was that loud noise?!

**This little guy looks scary and vicious...
I surrender...**

Fear is an emotion that we all experience. We fear tangible things like being hurt, robbed or cheated.

We also fear intangible things such as rejection, failure, success or public speaking. Fear can sometimes be useful, but it can also become your greatest enemy and hold your life in an awesome grip. Fear can keep you from going forward or experiencing the good things in life. Fear of failure often produces inaction.

"Let not your heart be troubled, neither let it be afraid"
<u>John 14:27</u>

🐾 Ask yourself : What's the worst that can happen? Most of the time your fear is imagined

🐾 Fear of failure often produces inaction

"Never be afraid to trust an unknown future to a known God"
Corrie ten Boom

"Fear not tomorrow, for God is already there"
Author Unknown

"I believe the greatest failing of all is to be frightened. When I look back on my life, all my mistakes have been made because I was afraid"
Kathrine Mansfield

Bunny's Wisdom:

- I caused my body unnecessary stress by being fearful of many things

- Don't let fear hold you back from what life has to offer

Definition of FEAR: False Evidence Appearing Real

HAVE FUN, EXPLORE NEW THINGS, LAUGH MORE

MAKE ENTHUSIASM PART OF YOUR LIFE

"A man can succeed in almost anything for which he has unlimited enthusiasm"
Charles Schwab

At Christmas time Bunny had fun with the rest of the family opening her gift, which usually was some doggie treat. She would tear the paper and would be anxious to see what surprise would come out. She did not need fancy things to be happy and have fun.

**Christmas is my favorite holiday,
I have so much fun opening my presents**

Do you like exploring new and exciting things and trying them out? Bunny did.

She was always curious to see what we were doing. Whenever we were working on a project, she would sit and watch us and participate. Our backyard has a hill which fills up with weeds after the rain. Anytime we worked on the hill she would "work" alongside us, pulling weeds and roots with her mouth. She would mimic whatever we were doing. She just couldn't stand being left out of anything that was going on.

When a friend gave my husband a little turtle for his birthday, Bunny followed that thing everywhere. She was fascinated by this new arrival. She had never seen a creature like that before and was thrilled to have a new playing companion. Another time a little frog jumped out of our pool, I have no idea how it had gotten there, and Bunny ran over and put it in her mouth, only to spit it out quicker than she had put it in. Apparently it did not taste very good. She ran around spitting for a while.

What on earth are you?
Go away from my yard or I will have you for Lunch!

🐕 Be excited about doing new things and experiencing new places

🐕 Choose challenge and change. There are endless opportunities

🐕 Be adventurous. You never know what it can lead you to

🐕 Be open to spontaneity, serendipity and surprise

🐾 *Bunny's Wisdom:*

● *Never miss an opportunity to leave the house and explore new smells*

● *Never pass up an opportunity to go for a joy ride*

● *I can spend hours smelling "stuff"*

I love the wind on my face................

Bunny also used to do some pretty funny things and used to make us laugh a lot. We teased her a lot and she played tricks on us as well. They say that laughter is the best medicine, so make it a point to take time to laugh. Actually, experts say that laughing can actually decrease pain, increase endorphins and lower blood pressure. Debi Di Sandro, author of *Tales of a Slightly off Supermom*, suggests taking a "chuckle" break as often as you take a coffee break. Even back in ancient times, the Spartans had figured out that cheerfulness, good humor, laughter and peace of mind are powerful elements to good health. They had dedicated a little statue to the "God of Laughter" in each of their eating halls.

> *"He will...fill your mouth with laughter and your lips with shouts of joy"*
> **Job 8:21**

> *"A cheerful heart is good medicine"*
> **Proverbs 17:22**

- 🐾 Rent a funny movie, watch a funny sitcom or tell a funny joke
- 🐾 Be cheerful and playful
- 🐾 Laugh out loud

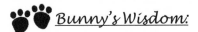 *Bunny's Wisdom:*

I make my family laugh a lot, it relieves stress

I don't think this is too funny!............

When Bunny was excited about something she couldn't hide it. She would wag her tail and run around in circles, run around the house, jump up and down. All it took was some extra energy, imagination, an old sock or a shoe, throwing her toys up in the air and then catching them or chasing after them. Of course, she always enjoyed parties, because she got lots of food and attention from all the guests. Her joy and enthusiasm brought a smile to my face.

> *"Without enthusiasm there is no progress in the world"*
> **Woodrow Wilson**

Are we excited about our job, family, friends, a hobby, a vacation coming up or anything else? Does our face show it ? People can see and sense our enthusiasm or lack of it.

Bunny's Wisdom:

- *It doesn't take much to make me happy. I'm always excited to see the same old people. All they have to do is leave the room for five minutes and come back*

- *When you are happy, dance around and wag your entire body*

- *Put enthusiasm in everything that you do*

- *Run, romp and play daily*

PRIORITIZE THE IMPORTANT THINGS IN YOUR LIFE

"We realize our dilemma goes deeper than the shortage of time; it is basically a problem of priorities. We confess, that we have left undone those things that we ought to have done; and we have done those things which we ought not to have done."

Charles E. Hummel

By observing Bunny's behavior I realized that she always did what seemed to be important to her and then give it her full attention, totally immersing herself in the moment. For example: if she was in the middle of her dinner or playing with her toys and we asked her if she wanted to go out for a walk, she would drop whatever she was in the middle of doing and take the walk. She would rather take the opportunity for a walk, no matter how long or short, than do her other activities. Obviously she always gave that a higher priority. Even at times when she was not feeling her best, she never passed up the opportunity to go for a walk.

It made me wonder if I was prioritizing what is important for my family and myself? Was I spending enough time with someone I love or was I doing chores that could wait. How many times had I passed up an opportunity to spend time with friends or family, because I had too many little chores that had to be done? Unfortunately I can never go back and recapture that time. I am ashamed to admit that sometimes I still waste time and energy doing a bunch of "unimportant" things while ignoring the more important. Why do we think being "busy" is a good thing? Today you hear everyone talking about having a "full plate." Have you ever wondered how many meaningful things we might be missing out on while we piddle around with our "full plates?"

🐕 Reduce the urgency that crowds your life and have a more meaningful participation in fewer activities

With the "busy-ness" of life, we seem to forget to stop and look at what is really important. Instead of going in "circles" why not take a pause to ask our-selves:

🐕 Is what I am doing now getting me closer to my family, my children, my friends, my dreams?

67

🐈 Is what I am doing now building relationships with the people who matter to me the most?

🐈 Is what I am doing now getting me closer to the life I want?

If we answered NO to any of these questions, maybe we need to sit down and re-examine our priorities.

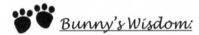 *Bunny's Wisdom:*

Do what is most important to you <u>first</u>, then come back and do the other things later

---

SHOW LOVE, LOYALTY AND COMMITMENT TO THE PEOPLE CLOSE TO YOU

"A dog is the only thing on earth that loves us more than he loves himself..."

<u>Anonymous</u>

Our pets represent all of the qualities man aspires to have. One of these qualities is that of loving unconditionally, without judging. Someone once said " we give dogs time we can spare, space we can spare and love we can spare. In return, dogs give us their "all." How true. That is the best deal man has ever had, isn't it? Our dogs love us no matter what we say or do. You can say the most foolish thing and your dog will give you a look that says "My God you're RIGHT, you're a GENIUS!" However, don't forget what Ann Landers once wrote: *"Don't accept your dog's admiration as conclusive evidence that you are wonderful."*

"Love is giving one another space to be all they are, and all that they are not"

Anonymous

Bunny used to greet us at the door with such enthusiasm, you would think she had not seen us for days, even if we were gone for a very short time.

They're home, they're home!!!
I missed them sooooo much........

If Bunny were a child she'd probably give us lots of hugs and kisses, just like little children do. Other times she would lick our face when we were sad and put her head on our lap, or just sit close and cuddle. The thing I remember the most is when she would look into your eyes and there was no question in my mind there was unconditional love.

"Let us love one another, for love comes from God"

1John 4:7

Wouldn't it be wonderful if we could all love this way? Unfortunately many people withhold affection because they are afraid to be rejected, or look foolish. They miss out on love!

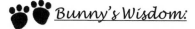 *Bunny's Wisdom:*

- *When loved ones come home, always run to greet them*
- *Sit close and cuddle*
- *Love your family unconditionally*

With love comes loyalty and commitment as well.

No matter how we treat our pets, they offer us unwavering loyalty. Although Bunny enjoyed visiting our friends and relatives, she always wanted to come home with us, no matter how much they fed her or how much they played with her.

"There is one element that is worth its weight in gold and that is loyalty. It will cover a multitude of weaknesses"

Phillip Armour

Bunny's wisdom:

Be loyal to your family, because they love you and take good care of you

> *"Lack of loyalty is one of the major causes of failure in every walk of life"*
> **Napoleon Hill**

She also showed commitment, by "protecting" our house. Not that she was a guard dog by any means. Actually, she was a scaredy-cat, but even so, she would bark at anybody knocking on our door. She was doing her "duty." We would tell her to "watch the house" anytime we were leaving and she would sit close to the door, or, if left outdoors, she would sit by the back gate until we would return.

GET AWAAAAAY.........................

Our loyalty and commitment for Bunny meant that we had to make some personal sacrifices through our time, energy and money. We always planned our trips and other events around Bunny's injections, since they were on a certain time every month. Sometimes we have to do these things for those we love. Of course, we must be careful whom we give our loyalty to, therefore, choose your friends wisely.

Whether it is getting a new puppy, raising a child, working on our marriage or our business, taking a class or any other project that we start, we must commit ourselves to it. We must not get excited with the "newness" of a "project," and then loose interest and give it up or abandon it later, half-finished.

Stay committed to anything you start to do and see it until it is finished!

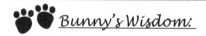 *Bunny's Wisdom:*

My parents and I are committed to each other 100 percent

**I don't know how this happened,
but it's my duty to raise them
and take care of them...**

SAVE FOR A RAINY DAY

YOU NEVER KNOW WHEN YOU MAY NEED THE MONEY

"It is not what comes into a man's hands that enriches him, but what he saves from slipping through them"

H. F. Kletzing

When we would give Bunny bones for her to lick, she would go outside and dig a hole to bury them. Many months later she would find the site through scent and dig them up. She knew exactly where they were.

As time passed and as she became weaker with age, she would still go through this ritual, but the holes were very shallow and the dirt would barely cover the bones. You could see all the little bones sticking out of the dirt. Another thing that she started to do was to try and "bury" her doggie treats in the house under the carpet. What I find fascinating is the dog's instinct to cache food, creating a reserve for time of need, which I understand is inherited from wolves. They continue to do it even in old age.

We also need to save for a rainy day. If we don't spend everything we earn all at once, but instead save some of it and maybe invest it, we will be happier later when we need it. All things cost money, don't they?

Bunny cost us thousands of dollars, and if we wanted to, we could have put her to sleep long ago. I am thankful that we didn't have to.

Don't waste all your treasures on foolish things. You don't know what tomorrow will bring. Having a reserve is always helpful.

- 🐕 Save and invest for tomorrow, don't spend all your money today

- 🐕 Don't become hostage to a lifestyle that is above your means

---

🐾 *Bunny's Wisdom:*

- *Remember to take some of your "doggie" bones and bury them for later*

- *I'm glad my "parents" had enough money to keep me going... I enjoyed my life*

I also believe that we should be good stewards of our money and we must be wise on how we handle money. If we spend a little less than we can afford, then we can build wealth. Building wealth does not depend on how much money we make or how much we spend, but rather, it depends on how much we save and how much we invest! Money is neither good or bad, it is how we use it that determines its value.

🐕 Work hard and make as much money as you can, when you can, because then you can help yourself and be a blessing to others

I need to save this bone for later...

PERSIST, PERSEVERE AND NEVER QUIT

"The will to persevere is often the difference between failure and success"

David Sarnoff

*W*hen Bunny wanted something she would first show us what she wanted. Then she would gradually start getting more assertive and finally she would start barking. Sometimes it was a snack, sometimes it was going for a walk, playing ball or getting a little back rub. Very seldom did she give up. If the door to a room was closed and we were there, she would scratch the door and bark until we would let her in. She never gave up. When she was digging for a bone she had previously buried she would dig with abandon until she would find the bone.

I won't stop until I find it...

Have you ever watched how persistently a spider spins its web, waiting for its prey? Learn to bear adversity, to persist in the face of hardship and use past disappointments to keep going, when you would rather quit. Everything that is worthwhile in life requires perseverance. It means you have to work for it. You may not see results right away, but it's OK. Just keep doing your thing.

"We also rejoice in our sufferings, because we know that suffering produces perseverance; perseverance, character; and character, hope"
Romans 5:3-4

Are you following your dreams? Or are you giving up too soon? Do you say to yourself I will do it, or do you say I can't do it? Do you say to yourself: Nobody in my family ever did this so why do I think

> *"Persistent people begin their success where others end in failure"*
> **Edward Eggleston**

that I can? Are you letting other people discourage you? Are you letting them tell you that you can't have, do or be something? Don't believe them. If you persist, in due time you will get what you want.

 Follow your dreams

 Don't quit, Don't give up, Keep going, Be Persistent!

Affirmation: "I can do anything I set my mind to."

Bunny's Wisdom:

- *If what you want lies buried, dig until you find it*

- *I can't eat a big bone all at once, but I can finish it by taking small bites*

80

FORGIVE

*"He that cannot forgive others
breaks the bridge over which he must pass
himself; for every man needs to be forgiven..."*
Edward Herbert

*M*any times Bunny got into things, such as: destroying plants, digging holes, chewing up carpet or stealing things from the kitchen counter. You name it she did it... (At least she tried it once). I would scold her and be angry with her. She would disappear for a while and hide and when she figured out I was over it, she would re-appear and be cute, cuddly and playful, as if nothing had happened. She didn't hold a 'grudge.' No scolding was too serious for immediate and joyful forgiveness. I realized that it didn't pay for me to stay upset and angry for too long either. I would 'forgive' her and move on.

"Forgiving is not forgetting, it's letting go of the past"
Mary McLeod Bethun(Educator) (Born 1875)

Why do we hold on to old hurts and grudges? It only kills us slowly inside and deprives us from a joyful life.

🐾 Forgive people, even if they have wronged you. Holding on to anger is like drinking poison and hoping the other person will die. Well, they don't. Most of the time they don't even know you are upset with them. They don't even know or think they did you wrong.

> *"Be kind and compassionate to one another, forgiving each other, even as in Christ, God forgave you"*
> **Ephesians 4:32**

🐾 Learn to forgive and let go of the past

🐾 Learn to live in the present

🐾 Stop blaming yourself and others

I don't know why it is so hard to forgive others. Especially, those who have hurt us deeply. I suppose we would forgive them if they were to ask for "forgiveness." But, if they don't ask, we don't give. Do we? Sometimes...not always. We should do it all the time!

> *"You must make allowances for each other's faults and forgive the person who offends you"*
> **Colossians 3:13**

Forgiveness continues to be at the research forefront. Medical researchers, psychologists and theologians unite in the belief that forgiveness is directly related to physical, emotional and spiritual health.

"You are emotionally healthy to the exact degree to which you can freely forgive others for anything they may have done that has hurt you in any way. The inability to forgive lies at the root of most unhappiness. It leads to feelings of guilt, resentment, anger, and hostility toward others"

Brian Tracy

 Bunny's Wisdom:

When you're scolded, don't pout for too long... run right back and make friends

A FRIEND DOES NOT ASK FOR ANYTHING IN RETURN

"A friend loves at all times"
Proverbs 17:17

Bunny made friends very easily. As a matter of fact, because of Bunny, my dad met a lot of people in our neighborhood. People would stop and comment what a cute face and pretty eyes Bunny had and would start a conversation. The kids would always stop and ask if they could pet her. They would ask: Does she bite? Can I pet her? What's her name? Bunny loved that!! Her ears would perk up and her tail would start wagging. She enjoyed the moment and the touch of these precious little children.

Most importantly Bunny was our best friend. She knew when we were happy and when we were sad. She was company to us. We enjoyed just having her there. She would give us little kisses. We would give her hugs and kisses too. Nothing complicated. We would just "hang out" with each other. Bunny would just sit there and look at you with her big brown eyes as if to say: " I will always be your friend. Don't worry about anything."

With a friend, silence is comfortable, laughter is sincere and conversation is meaningful. A friend is someone we can depend on and share ourself with, without being afraid of being judged. As friends we respect our differences and encourage growth in each other. You are there for your friend and your friend is there for you. A friend does not ask for anything in return.

- Send a little note or make a five-minute phone call just to ask "how's it going?" Sometimes that's all it takes to make someone know you care

- Invite a friend over for lunch or a spur of the moment dinner. Things don't always have to be perfectly planned to enjoy the company of a friend

- Listen patiently to complaints and tears, and reach out to offer understanding, encouragement and reassurance

> *"The reason a dog has so many friends is that he wags his tail instead of his tongue."*
> **Anonymous**

<u>Bunny's Wisdom:</u>

- When someone is having a bad day, be silent, sit close by and nuzzle

- I always greet my friends and family with lots of kisses

- Thrive on attention and let people touch you

HAVE FAITH AND BELIEVE THAT ALL THINGS ARE POSSIBLE

"Faith is an important foundation for accomplishment"
A. M. Nelson

It took Bunny a long time to figure out how to open the door from the den to come out to the kitchen. It certainly was not that complicated. All she had to do was push a little harder. We'd be on the other side calling her "Come on, Bunny, you can do it!" For some reason, she had no faith in herself that she could come through. Finally, one day the breakthrough came. Once, she figured it out, she never again had a problem with it.

Don't you feel that sometimes we are so close to a breakthrough and yet we can't see it because of our lack of belief or faith in ourselves? Success can be right around the corner and yet we worry and can't believe it can happen to us. Even if we don't know what's behind that "door" or that we are capable of "opening" the "door," we must have faith. Without faith we lose all hope.

> "For a renewal of faith, look into the eyes of a child"
> **Kathryn Major**

Another form of faith came to me every time Bunny was ill and close to dying (and that happened several times). I would pray that the doctor would know to do the right thing. I knew that things would be in God's hands. I learned to think positive thoughts and have faith that this too was temporary and she would recuperate. Most circumstances in our lives are temporary. If you have faith you can overcome many hurdles.

🐾 Practice self-affirmations every day to keep your perspective positive and uplifting

Affirmation: "No matter what comes my way today, I will handle it"

My father-in-law always kept a sign on his desk that read: **Don't Worry, It May Never Happen!**

> "Faith is the substance of things hoped for, the evidence of things unseen..."
> **The Bible**

 _Bunny's Wisdom:_

Once I believed I could do it, I did. You can too

KEEP YOUR PROMISES

"A promise made is a debt unpaid"
Shakespeare

There were times when we were too tired to take Bunny for a walk or play with her. We would tell her "later." Well, she would come over and bug us all day. When we wouldn't do it, you could tell she would lay down with a sigh and look sad. She probably felt betrayed (if dogs can feel that!) because we had deliberately let her down and had lied to her.

After a while I learned not to say—maybe later. I would just tell her "NO, not today Bunny." She would go away pouting for a while, but she knew not to expect to go out that day.

- 🐕 Don't make promises you know you cannot keep

- 🐕 Don't tell people what they want to hear, knowing that you will never fulfill that promise. (Have you ever done that to your kids or people you interact with? How do you feel when others do it to you?)

🐈 Don't over promise and under deliver, always, under promise and over deliver

🐈 Always do what you say you are going to do

 Bunny' Wisdom:

- *I feel let down when they promise to take me for a walk and they don't do it*

- *If you are not planning to play with me, just say so*

LIVE YOUR LIFE SO THAT YOU WILL HAVE NO REGRETS

"Be very careful how you live, not as unwise but as wise, making the most of every opportunity"
Ephesians 5:15-16a:

Bunny made the most of the days when she felt her best. I am glad she did, because there were days when she wasn't up to it. We made it a point to do things with her when she was well. Even so, we still had a few regrets. We wish we had taken more pictures of Bunny along the way. We wish we had taken her to the beach for a walk. We wish we had taken her to her favorite park more often. We wish we had thought of taking some water for her on our long walks. We wish, we wish, we wish…

Just do what you want to do a little along the way and don't put things off. There will never be a "perfect" moment. Don't put yourself in a position where you look back and say, "I wish I had." Instead be in a position to say, "I'm glad I did." Do not procrastinate.

Are **you** putting things off for that "perfect" moment?

- Are you telling your family you love them?
- Are you spending enough time with the ones you love?
- Do you visit with your elderly parents and relatives?
- Have you made amends with someone who hurt you?
- Are you taking the trips you want to?
- Are you taking opportunities that come your way?
- Are you following your dreams?

The list is endless and personal to each one of us.

Whatever it is, we all have regrets. The important thing is seeing to it that they are as few as possible. They could be small things, but when not done, they can bother you for the rest of your life.

> *Do it NOW! Do it when you can...Don't wait!*
> *There could come a time when you won't be able to.*

Bunny's Wisdom:

- *Any trip is better than the one I didn't take*

- *Take a walk when you can*

Oh Dear...She spotted the CAT!!

REWARD YOURSELF
FOR YOUR
ACCOMPLISHMENTS

s I mentioned earlier, Bunny liked digging holes, and had a keen sense of smell. We always had trouble with gophers in our backyard and at two different occasions, Bunny caught a gopher. Boy, she was so proud of that. She couldn't wait to show us. She had it in her mouth and wanted to bring it into the house. We couldn't pry it from her mouth. She wanted to keep it and show it off. Finally, we took it away and told her she was a "good girl" and rewarded her with a few doggie biscuits. She was so excited about what she had done. Then, a few days later she caught another one. That was for sure the highlight of her day. After that we would call her our "hunting dog." Other times she would alert us to opossums, and skunks or she would chase away cats. She would feel so proud of herself, as if to say "I did a good job."

How many times do we accomplish good things, but put them aside as not being a "big deal"? If you cannot celebrate and reward yourself with the little successes along the way, you will not know what to do when the bigger ones come along. God has given all of us different talents and abilities. We must accept ourselves and turn our focus on what is right with us. Instead of criticizing our faults, we must learn to trust our skills. We must reach our potential by amplifying our good qualities, and shedding our weaker traits in the process. We must also help others do the same.

Ask yourself if your expectations of the people you interact/live with are so high that you never stop to reward them when they accomplish little things. Sometimes that is all they may be capable of doing.

Do you encourage someone when you see what they do best? Your encouragement will motivate them to do more and they will feel good about themselves. How about you? Are you savoring **your** victories?

- Be proud and celebrate your accomplishments, no matter how simple or small they may seem
- Acknowledge your accomplishments and pamper yourself with simple pleasures:
  - a new dress
  - a piece of chocolate mousse
  - a trip to the movies
  - a trip to the beach
  - a massage

Bunny's Wisdom:

- When I catch the gopher, I enjoy the victory
- I work hard, play hard and rest well

DOG DAYS OF SUMMER

Aaaah...there is nothing like relaxing by the pool after putting in a long day in the yard...

TAKE A BREAK AND MAKE TIME FOR SOLITUDE

"The best thinking has been done in solitude. The worst has been done in turmoil"

T. Edison

Bunny would go and take breaks (of course, I think cats and dogs do that a lot). She had her favorite spots where she would go just to be away from everybody and take a little snooze. Just imagine if we wouldn't let her. She probably would have been nasty and growl at us. But after she had her rest, she would reappear and be lovable.

Don't you think you and I are the same? How do you feel at the end of a long day. Do you feel like having a conversation or doing "one more thing" that someone in your family asks you to do? NO. You feel irritable, grouchy, tired etc. Probably not fun to be around.

We often think that down-time is unproductive and that taking a nap once in a while would translate into "laziness." That is the furthest thing from the truth. It's OK to take a break. It will recharge you. Animals don't work non-stop. They take time out and rest. You will not be good to anybody when you don't feel good because you are run down.

🐕 Take care of yourself , relax, take a nap. It can be in the middle of the day, when you get home from work or whenever you can

🐕 Find a comfortable balance between motion and rest

It's nice to be away from all the commotion...

We are constantly bombarded with visual stimulation, noise and the demands of others. But, we were not designed to handle this amount of stimuli. Solitude can be a good thing. Solitude is like food. Sometimes you need a real big meal; sometimes you just need a snack. The need to be alone varies for everyone, but experts agree that it is a basic requirement to a clear mind.

> *"It is when a man is alone, away from the influence of other men, that he can work on himself. It is in solitude that he must correct his thoughts, driving out the bad and stimulating the good"*
>
> **Leo Tolstoy**

Stealing time for solitude reduces stress, improves creativity and lets you recharge your relationships. Our busy schedules can complicate our lives and make your time not your own. Sometimes we need some peace and quiet to listen to ourselves, before we can listen to everyone else.

🐾 Learn to delight in the peace of simplicity and the quite space of solitude

🐾 "Stop," just as you would press "pause" on your VCR, and enjoy a moment of idle time

> *"On the 7th day, He rested from all his work"*
>
> **Genesis 2:2**

Bunny's Wisdom:

- *On a warm day, stop to lie on your back on the grass*
- *On hot days, drink lots of water and lie under a shady tree*
- *Take naps*

*"Every now and then go away,
have a little relaxation,
for when you come back to your work
your judgment will be surer."*
Leonardo Da Vinci

WHEN WE TEACH
WE LEARN

*"Learning is a treasure which will
follow its owner everywhere"*
Chinese Proverb

*W*e taught our dog many things, like most people do; such as potty training, where to sleep, when to eat, how to catch ball and some other tricks. She was a good student. She learned well. However, I think I learned more from her just by watching and observing her, and trying to figure out what she wanted. After a while, I learned to understand what she wanted by her behavior and mannerisms. For example: when she wanted me to pet her or give her a little back rub she would put her paw on my hand and pull it. When she wanted us to rub her belly she would roll over on her back and expose her belly. When she wanted to go to the patio she would reach up and scratch the door, and if we didn't respond, she would give a little woof. If she was eating and you wanted to pet her or tease her, she would get pretty defensive. Anytime we would approach her bowl, she would give a little growl, to warn us to stay away.

We taught each other and learned from each other. However, among the most important things I learned from Bunny were: patience, tolerance, kindness, appreciation, loyalty, love, compassion, commitment and how to be observant, attentive and unselfish...

🐈 Be a life-long learner. Engage in daily self-renewal

Knowledge comes from different sources, sometimes from areas you least expect. It is very rewarding to be a teacher to others but it is as rewarding when we allow ourselves to also be a student. The mind is like a parachute and it can only work if we open it. Open it to new ideas and information. That is how we grow. And knowledge is the only thing that nobody can take away from us. Learning is a life long process. Every day is a new day which brings us new lessons.

**OK, now that I mastered this trick,
will it be long before I get my biscuit?**

"To teach is to learn"
<u>**Japanese proverb**</u>

*"Anyone who stops learning is old, whether at twenty
or eighty. Anyone who keeps learning stays young.
The greatest thing in life is to keep your mind young"*
<u>**Henry Ford**</u>

Bunny's Wisdom:

- *I like learning new tricks, it stimulates my mental well-being*

- *Learn your lessons well and you will be rewarded*

> **"If you stop learning, you will forget what you already know."**
> **Proverbs 19:27**

SEASONS IN OUR LIVES

*"Give people flowers
when they can smell them"*
Nicholas Caussin

There is a life cycle to all living things. A season, if you will, when puppies are young, cute, cuddly, playful and full of energy. Enjoy that time with them. Play and be joyful and let yourself go like a child. That will not last forever. As a little puppy grows older, she no longer has the energy she used to have (just like people). Arthritis sets in, her facial hair is getting whiter, she has bad breath, her joints hurt and she cannot jump on the couch or catch a frizbee, like she used to. She has incontinence problems and she starts to have less and less appetite. She doesn't want to play anymore. You can tell that she mentally wants to, but physically she can't. Her walks are shorter and shorter and less frequent.

Then one day she is gone. Love her and be with her a little everyday. Don't wait! Be thankful for all the beautiful times you had with her. Take lots of pictures along the way.

Bunny was hard of hearing the last year of her life and would sleep very soundly. In the morning she did not want to get up. She wanted to sleep in longer and longer. My husband would play a little game with her, until she would get up. He would shuffle his feet and go to the door and finally she would follow. Some mornings I would go over to her and give her a little hug and a kiss and she would wake up from a deep sleep with a confused look, as if she did not know where she was. These are the little things we remember.

The same applies to the people in our lives.

🐕 Do things with people when they are still alive and able. One day they will be gone and you'll wish you had

___

🐾 *Bunny's Wisdom:*

- *Enjoy life to the fullest, one day at a time*

- *I played ball when I was young and watched TV when I got older*

- *I made lasting memories with my" human" family*

___

There are seasons to life and there is a right time for each season. The beauty of life is trying to enjoy these seasons of our lives.

*"There is a time for everything
and a season for every activity
under heaven..."*

A time to be born and a time to die,
A time to plant and a time to uproot,
A time to kill and a time to heal,
A time to tear down and a time to build,
A time to weep and a time to laugh,
A time to mourn and a time to dance,
A time to scatter stones
and a time to gather them,
A time to embrace and a time to refrain,
A time to search and a time to give up,
A time to keep and a time to throw away,
A time to tear and a time to mend,
A time to be silent and a time to speak,
A time to love and a time to hate,
A time for war and a time for peace
Ecclesiastes 3:1-22

THERE COMES A TIME WHEN WE MUST "LET GO"

Sometimes we hold on to things and people for our own selfish reasons. It was very hard for us seeing Bunny ill and ready to die. We kept telling her to hang on a little longer. She kept bouncing back. But as her health kept deteriorating, we knew she had to go. We dreaded the thought that we would have to possibly have to ask the doctor to put her down. We constantly prayed that she would pass away on her own while we were home. As dreadful as the thought was, we had started to accept it. One day she ran upstairs with me and as she came up the last step she collapsed. She had done that before. Her legs would give out at unexpected times. She would not be able to get up for a while and then she would be OK again. Finally that day, I looked at her and tears started down my cheeks. I sat next to her and said "Bunny" it's OK, it is time for you to go, I don't want you to suffer any more. It was time for me to let go, even when it hurt so badly.

I don't know if she knew what I was talking about, but she sat with me and looked me in the eye, with her big brown beautiful eyes. I gave her some water and we sat there together for a long while. I held her in my arms and gave her a little kiss. After a while she was able to get up and walk downstairs.

That evening she was not well, she was very restless, couldn't sleep. We slept with her downstairs.

When my husband gave her her pills, she spit them out about a foot and a half, as if to say: "No more medication for me again!"

The next morning around 6 a.m. my husband let her go out to the backyard and was waiting for her by the door. She fell down and couldn't get up. He called me and told me to bring her bed. We put her on her bed and carried her inside. We stayed with her and comforted her until she passed away 20 minutes later.

There comes a time when we have to let go. A relationship, a loved one with a terminal illness, a job…

Bunny's Wisdom:

- *I hung around as long as I could, but there came a time for both of us to let go*

- *Appreciate the memories and move on*

FINDING COMFORT IN HEALING FROM LOSS AND SORROW

"Then shall the dust return to the earth as it was; and the spirit shall return unto God who gave it"

The Bible

No matter when death arrives, it always seems too soon. Doesn't it?

When Bunny died, I felt a physical pain in my heart that I cannot explain. She was a great loss to me.

She had been a companion to us , a friend, a play buddy and a confidant when we had a problem.

Death is so final. When it comes, it's over. Nothing you can do about it. It's finished. You cannot take back anything you said or did. You cannot give anything nor do anything you wish you had. Death closes the doors on plans and possibilities. Death ends all the stories we have yet to tell.

For the living, the loss is wrenching and the void devastating. It took several weeks before we stopped crying and feeling this horrible sense of loss. We grieved for a long time and even now after 5 years, we get teary-eyed thinking about her. According to some experts, crying relieves pent-up emotions, cleans out our minds and re-energizes the body. It's OK to cry once in a while and give your tears a nudge. Let yourself go.

Although we have had other pets in our lives, Bunny had touched us on a higher level, for different reasons. I believe she came into our lives for a reason and she fulfilled her purpose. We just had a special bond with her. When she died my husband saw her spirit, a little white cloud, go up as it left her little body. Unfortunately, I didn't see it. I was too busy crying and talking to her, trying to comfort her.

The next couple of nights we felt her presence in our bedroom. She came and set down by my side and then got up and plopped herself down on my husband's side as she used to do when she would come in to go to sleep. She would always take turns sleeping next to both of us. I knew it was her spirit. I heard paw steps coming in the room and then felt her lie down. I thought I was imagining things, and frankly, I was pretty spooked. I knew I wasn't sleeping, it wasn't a dream. I asked my husband if he heard anything and he said, "yes, I can feel Bunny's presence." (I remember my mother who had been very close to our dog, Lucky, tell me that when he passed away, years ago, she had felt him by her bed, and she was too scared to look and had pulled the sheets over her head). For several days after that incident both of us would wake up in the middle of the night. We were so conditioned in letting Bunny out several times during the night.

I know she is somewhere out there. Wherever little doggies go. Perhaps she is in "doggie heaven", because to us she was a little angel. I never felt this way before for anybody, even a parent, relative or friend. I cannot explain it. I know it sounds weird. With time our pain is healed and our love endures in the solace of our memories. I read somewhere, that Will Rogers once said: "If there are no dogs in Heaven, then when I die, I want to go where they went." How sweet. I bet he had a wonderful dog in his lifetime.

Some people believe that everything on earth is a picture, or pattern of things in heaven. Since God promises that he will not withhold any good thing from those who love him, then why wouldn't he let us have the animals we loved on earth, with us in heaven? If God can raise the dead and recreate our loved ones from dust and ashes, why wouldn't he restore our beloved pets too?

We cling to the promise of life everlasting. Maybe we shall be together again...

Bye Bye Bunny... We love you, we miss you. You will always have a special place in our hearts. You were a good little girl. You came into our lives when we needed it the most.

"You think dogs won't be in heaven? I tell you, they will be there long before any of us."

Robert Louis Stevenson

THE TEN COMMANDMENTS OF OUR PETS

1. My life is likely to last 10 to 15 years. Any separation from you will be painful for me. Remember that before you adopt me.

2. Give me time to understand what you want from me.

3. Place your trust in me — it is crucial to my well being.

4. Don't be angry with me for long and don't lock me up as punishment. You have your work, your entertainment and your friends. I have only you.

5. Talk to me sometimes. Even if I don't understand your words, I do understand your voice when it is speaking to me.

6. Be aware that however you treat me, I'll never forget it.

7. Remember before you hit me that I have teeth that could easily crush the bones in your hand, but that I choose not to bite you!

8. Before you scold me for being uncooperative, obstinate or lazy, ask yourself if something might be bothering me. Perhaps I'm not getting the right food or I've been out in the sun too long, or my heart is getting old and weak.

9. Take care of me when I get old—you too will grow old.

10. Go with me on difficult journeys. Never say I can't bear to watch it or let it happen in your absence. *"Everything is easier for me if you are there. Remember, I LOVE you.*

~ **Anonymous**

TRIBUTES FROM FRIENDS

Always in your heart. She sleeps, perhaps she dreams of the many hugs and little kindnesses you gave her. My prayer is that you can often find that little puppy, right there in your memory, dancing and wagging her tail.

I can see little glimpses of her requisite inspections and hospitality at your front door. I know you miss her greatly. Please accept my sympathy.

Rick

My heart is with you. Our pets become part of the family and when they leave us it is a painful loss. That empty hole takes a long time to heal to a level of being able to bear it without tears. My dog Casey has been gone for a couple of years and I still miss him terribly. I do hope I get to see him again one day. And that's my prayer for you. That you will see Bunny again all healthy and playful and stay with you throughout eternity.

May the good Lord above help to ease your sorrow and may the joys and love Bunny gave you and your family remain sweet memories in your heart.

Scilia

I'm so sorry about your doggy… I know you dearly loved that dog and they are family. Only when you are lucky enough to have the one special dog can you begin to understand. It leaves a big void. Nothing or no one loves you as unconditionally as your dog. I'm soooooooooooo sorry, Sofia. I hope she didn't suffer a lot. We lost our dog, Thesa, 3 years ago and we still tear up when we share stories about her or look at her pictures.

Just wanted to say how sorry I am an let you know I am thinking about you.

Karlee

There must be a heaven for the animal friends we love. They are not human, yet they bring out our humanity…sometimes in ways that other people cannot. They do not worry about fame or fortune… instead they bring our hearts nearer to the joy of simple things. Each day they teach us little lessons in trust and steadfast affection. Whatever heaven may be, there is surely a place in it for friends as good as these.

Anyone who has loved a pet can understand your loss. May it help to know how much others care.

Patty and Randy

APPENDIX 1

Pets are a Part of Your Family

As your pets guardian, you have the responsibility to make careful, educated decisions about his or her well-being.

One of the things I would strongly recommend is that you take your pet to the vet for regular check-ups. If you suspect any health problems take them to the veterinary specialist immediately so that they can be diagnosed properly. Unfortunately, the dog or puppy cannot tell us what is wrong, they rely on our observations. There are websites on-line that provide useful information about dog illness symptoms. *These are not intended to be used to diagnose or treat a sick dog, but what they do is give you information on the symptoms and their possible causes.* One of these websites is called "Dog Symptoms Sorter" and it lists all the different symptoms in alphabetical order.

To access the Website go to: www.dog-names.org.uk. Click on "Canine dog health" and then scroll down to "Dog Health Problems" and click on "Dog sickness symptoms sorter."

You may also want to check out other on-line canine support groups.

What is Addison's Disease?

Addison's Disease, also known as hypoadreno-corticism, is an insufficient production and secretion of a hormone called corticosteroid by the adrenal gland cortex. This hormone is very important in maintaining the balance of two minerals in the blood: sodium and potassium. In Addison's Disease the sodium levels are too low and potassium levels are too high.

Addison's disease is a life threatening condition that must be treated ASAP. Untreated dogs are usually dead within 24 hours from heart failure brought on by the increased potassium levels.

Dr. Thomas Addison first described the disease in humans in 1849. In 1856 it was demonstrated that removal of both adrenal glands resulted in death of experimental animals. This proved that these glands are necessary for maintenance of life. Addison's Disease in dogs was not reported until 1953.

What causes the disease?

Most cases occur naturally. The adrenal glands may stop working for a number of reasons including:

- A genetic defect or a genetic predisposition
- Sudden removal of Cortisone therapy. Steroids are frequently used to treat

dogs for various illnesses and their use diminish the dog's ability to produce its own steroids. As a result, if the steroid medication is suddenly stopped, it can take some time for the dog to produce enough itself. Therefore it is important that steroids are withdrawn gradually.

🐕 After the dog has been through a major stress situation. If the dog has an impaired tolerance to stress, even mild physical or emotional stress can cause an Addisonian crisis. A healthy dog responds to stress by releasing cortisol, an Addisonian dog cannot do this.

What constitutes stress and the amount of stress a dog can tolerate varies with each dog. Examples of stressors are: elective surgery such as spaying/ neutering, traumatic injuries, infection, vaccinations, cold weather, or psychological distress such as trips to the vet, the family packing up for vacation, being placed in a boarding kennel, traveling, summer thunderstorms or fireworks. Stress can also be induced by fun things such as taking an obedience class.

What is an Addisonian Crisis?

The dog appears to have had no previous illness and suddenly becomes very ill. The owner has to pay close attention to these dogs by watching for signs and symptoms and changes in the dog's behavior. These dogs crash quickly! Okay in the evening but by morning all signs and symptoms are present. Symptoms that can alert the owners to a problem are: dehydration (touch the dog's gums, if they feel tacky this is a sign of dehydration, a well-hydrated dog has wet slippery gums,) changes in appetite, vomiting and/or diarrhea, appear tired and there is no tail wagging. Typically the dog is unable to stand or move about at all. Unlike a seizure, the dog can lose consciousness. Dogs experiencing the Addisonian crisis are genuine emergencies and must be taken to the vet immediately and must receive immediate care or they will die. Emergency care includes the administration of large volumes of intravenous fluids (sodium and chloride) and corticosteroids.

Who gets Addison's Disease?

Addison's Disease can occur in dogs of any age, sex or breed. It has occurred to dogs as early as 12 weeks of age. However, current research has shown that 70% diagnosed are young to middle aged females. 80% are 7 years of age or younger with the average age being 4.6 years.

What are the symptoms?

The following are commonly reported symptoms. Severity can vary from dog to dog.

- Anorexia
- Weight Loss
- Vomiting/diarrhea
- Weakness
- Collapse
- Shaking and shivering
- Excessive urination with or without excessive thirst
- Fatigue
- Increased thirst
- The dog may also appear clumsy and unable to climb stairs or jump on the bed. This may be due to muscle loss or weakness. The dog does not have the strength to do normal activities.

Unfortunately many of these symptoms can be confused with other diseases, such as kidney failure, acute renal disorders and gastrointestinal disorders.

Is the disease treatable?

If caught early enough, it is controllable with an excellent prognosis. After therapy stabilizes the condition, the dog usually leads a normal life with few if any restrictions. The most important factors are long-term response to medication and diligent owners and veterinarians. Recognition of the disease and the cost of treatment seem to be the biggest obstacles to a successful outcome.

What is the treatment?

Once the dog is diagnosed the vet will try to stabilize the dog on Florinef in pill form which has been used for over 20 years. It is taken once or twice a day.

The other method (DOCP) is an injection that is given once every 21-30 days. Dogs on this medication may also require a cortisone supplementation. Such supplements include prednisone or prednisolone.

The vet regularly reevaluates the animal to see if the medication dosage needs adjusting. The medication is individualized to the severity of the condition and the patient response. The tests used to evaluate and diagnose adrenal gland disease are an ACTH test and electrolyte tests for sodium/potassium levels.

Long-term management

One side effect that requires caution is immune system suppression. This can lead to compromised resistance and susceptibility to infections. Otherwise, your dog can lead a normal, long life while on the prescribed medication.

APPENDIX 2

Doesn't Your Best Friend Deserve Some Pampering and the Best Care?

Here are some common tips:

Shiny fur and clean skin is not a luxury but a well maintained appearance is an outward sign of a healthy and happy pet and so is white clean teeth.

Taking a Bath

Nowadays, there are so many wonderful products on the market with herbal scents and oils to moisturize the skin and coat. A variety of shampoos have vitamin A and E which help eliminate dry skin, smell fresh and clean.

- Make sure you check shampoo labels to pick the one that will be best for your dog
- Plan to wash them once a month (if too often it can take out oil from skin)
- Make sure you rinse the shampoo out of their coat thoroughly to prevent itching
- Protect their ears from getting wet
- Make it a fun experience-be prepared to get wet

🐕 Once you dry them fully brush them from head to tail

Show those pearly whites

As if bad breath isn't enough reason, consider that 80% of dogs develop periodontal diseases by the time they are 5 years old.

Healthy teeth and gums may be among the most important aspects of an animal's survival. Without them your pet cannot eat properly, groom herself, or protect herself from danger. While you should schedule yearly check-ups at the veterinarian, routine home care is also very important.

Be sure to keep an eye out for indications of possible dental disease: bad breath, excessive drooling, difficulty chewing, loss of appetite and loose teeth. If any of these problems persist, check with the vet for treatment.

Bunny's veterinarian taught us how to care for her teeth, although she never was too fond of the experience.

🐕 Brush your dog's teeth regularly, daily if possible, but once a week at least

🐕 Get your pet used to your touch by massaging her mouth and gums with your fingertips

🐕 Gradually start to brush her teeth and gums with a toothbrush and toothpaste made for pets (ask your vet.) Never use a human toothbrush or toothpaste—it is harmful to pets.

🐕 Give your dog chew toys designed to clean teeth. Chewing rawhide has been shown to reduce plaque and tartar up to 25 percent.

Nutrition/Supplements

The right nutrition will give your pet more energy and help them maintain a healthy weight. Try a brand that contains essential vitamins, minerals, fruits and vegetables, including a balanced blend of Omega 6 and Omega 3 fatty acids.

I also believe that vitamins can make a difference, as well.

Flea and tick prevention

For your dog springtime brings in fleas and ticks leading to a potential skin irritation, health issues and home infestation. Take precautions early at the start of the season and before flea and tick populations multiply.

To check for fleas, run your fingers through your pet's fur, spreading the fur so that you can see down to the skin. There you might see "flea dirt", a dust that is actually flea excrement. You can also comb through your pet's fur with a wire brush, looking for fleas and flea dirt. Also look for the black, gritty dust in areas of your house where your pet has been lying down.

There are many flea and tick products available for your pet, and they work in different ways. Those that offer immediate relief usually kill adult fleas on contact or when fleas or ticks bite, but they don't harm the larvae or sterilize any remaining adults. When shopping, look for a product that protects your pet from both adult fleas and ticks, but also from flea eggs and larvae.

One of the products that we used for Bunny was a pill she took once a month. This kept fleas and ticks away from her. It really worked. Ask your vet about pills that will repel fleas and ticks. I really think it is worth it. It will relieve your pet from scratching and itching.

Make your outdoors and indoors flea and tick proof

Though inside is where you really want your house to be pest-free, outside is where you'll find your first line of defense. Flea larvae need to be in a humid environment and out of direct sunlight. Trimming lawns and weeds can help create an undesirable environment for flea larvae since there is less shade to hide in. There are also products that can be used to decrease outdoor populations of these pests even further.

To prevent and control fleas and ticks indoors make sure you vacuum floors and furniture surfaces as often as you can, together with a regular schedule of washing pet bedding and furniture coverings to remove immature stages of eggs and larvae.

You can also use flea and tick home products. Sprays kill fleas, ticks and flea eggs (as well as roaches, silverfish, earwigs, ants and other insects) on contact. One treatment works for up to 7 months and they are perfect for use on carpet, rugs, upholstery and pet bedding.

Taking some of these steps will treat your home, attack the environment and most importantly protect your pet.

Pet Health Care Insurance

You love your pet. You want her to get the best care when she gets sick or hurt. If possible try to get health insurance for your pet. There are companies that offer affordable coverage for emergency and major medical care, plus routine procedures such as neutering and vaccinations. Some may even help with prescriptions and lab fees.

Unfortunately, I never thought I would need it and when I did need it for Bunny, it was too late. She could not be insured because of her pre-existing condition.

We buy insurance for our cars, homes and our own health care…why not health insurance for our pets? If nothing else, it will give us peace of mind! Be proactive, in case you will ever need it later.

For Your Information

Check out *Reader's Digest*, May 2005 issue, for more information on the **Hydration System Dog Pack** by Outward Hound. It's a backpack that holds water, and your dog wears it like a vest. He can carry his own water supply on hikes or long walks.